EILEEN W. BARNES AWARD ANTHOLOGY

Saturday's Women

Edited & with Introduction by
Charlotte Mandel

Co-editors
Maxine Silverman, Rachel Hadas

Cover by Coco Gordon

SATURDAY PRESS
1982

Copyright © 1982 by Saturday Press
First Edition.

Acknowledgements:
Some of the poems in this book are reprinted with permission of the following publications in which they first appeared:
Arts in Society, "Somewhere in Erie, Pennsylvania"; *Herself,* "Rematch"; *Virginia Quarterly Review,* "The Egrets"; *The Georgia Review,* "Sustenance"; *Tar River Poetry,* "The Hinge"; *The Chowder Review,* "Maria Bonnifemme Died in 1672," "Job's Wife" (in shorter version; also reprinted in *Phoenix Rising); Intro 12,* "Their Marriage/Memory"; *Shadowgraphs,* "Constellation" (under title "The Dead Girl"); *Beloit Poetry Journal,* "Eve Names the Animals"; *Central Park,* "Some Things You Can't Forget"; *Escarpments,* "Spring on the Frontier"; *Bachy,* "Father That You Haven't Been Mine"; *Buckle,* "After 41 Years, I Find a Window in My Table"; *Connections,* "Child in Flight"; *Poetry View,* "War Games"; *The Dalhousie Review,* "End of Memory"; *Southern Poetry Review,* "Milk"; *Woman Poet: The Midwest,* "Deer in the Open Field"; *Poetry,* "The Crybaby at the Library" (copyright Modern Poetry Association); *Pig Iron,* "Aunt Mattie Dying"; *Yankee,* "Illuminations: Fish"; *Hiram Poetry Review,* "Fire Kites"; *Audit/Poetry,* "Learning the Ropes. Evanston, 1949"; *Blue Buildings,* "How Was I To Know"; *Hawaii Review,* "In a Wheat Field Mapped Like Kansas" (also reprinted as Water Mark Press Broadside); *The Louisville Review,* "The Voyage Out"; *M'Godolim,* "Our Stories"; *Pikestaff Forum,* "The War Came to Illinois"; *Alembic,* "The Farm: Blue Morning Light"; *Poet and Critic,* "Ride Up the Mountain"; *Voices of the Atlantic,* "Heartwood."

No part of this book may be reproduced without permission.

Library of Congress Cataloging in Publication Data

Main entry under title:

Saturday's women.

1. American poetry—Women authors. 2. American poetry—20th century. I. Mandel, Charlotte, date. II. Silverman, Maxine. III. Hadas, Rachel. IV. Saturday Press (Montclair, N.J.)
PS589.S25   1982   811'.54'08   82-10278
ISBN 0-938158-02-3 (pbk.)

Typeset by Ed Hogan and Leora Zeitlin
Aspect Composition
13 Robinson St., Somerville, Mass. 02145

SATURDAY PRESS
P. O. Box 884
Upper Montclair, N.Y. 07043

Contents

Introduction / Charlotte Mandel   6

Sheila Cowing / Sustenance   11
Patricia Hooper / Milk   12
Sandra Demarest / Running Away   13
Phyllis K. Collier / Trapping Gophers   14
Patricia Dobler / Their Marriage/Memory   16
Shelley Ehrlich / Job's Wife   17
Ghita Orth / Elephants—A Mythology   19
Carol R. Hackenbruch / Far From The Lake Without Foghorn   20
Mary Kay Rummel / How One Leaves The Order   21
Sheila Cowing / The Hinge   25
Anneliese Wagner / Our Stories   26
Coco Gordon / Father That You Haven't Been Mine   27
Susan Donnelly / Eve Names The Animals   28

June Rachuy Brindel / The Poet's Daimon   30
Norma Westwood / Seated, The Body Feels As If   32
Caroline Knox / The Crybaby At The Library   33
Elaine Dallman / Maria Bonnifemme Died in 1672   35
Katherine Wells / Ask The Child About Religion   36
Ann Woolfolk / Twister   37
Barbara Ewell / Riverview Hotel For Women   38
Anne Harter-Jones / Why Do They Keep A Canary   41
LoVerne Brown / Rematch   43
Francine Ringold / How Was I To Know   44
Lisa Ress / Grandmother's House: The Baba Yaga   45
Roberta Chester / Heartwood   46
Ruth F. Eisenberg / Some Things You Can't Forget   47
Jean Hollander / A Journalist Interviews Two Women
                    In Cambodia   48
Ann Z. Leventhal / Snapshot   50
Ellin Carter / Two-Dimensional Recall   51
Phebe Hanson / Sturdy Arms   52
Lois V. Walker / The War Came To Illinois   53
Lisa Ress / Learning The Ropes. Evanston, 1949   54
Elizabeth Anne Socolow / Cityscape   55
Susan Donnelly / Constellation   56
Barbara Winder / Ride Up The Mountain   57
Elizabeth Williams / The Sunbathers   58
Barbara Langham / Aunt Mattie Dying   60
Jeanne Elliott / My Mother's Poetry Circle   60
Nancy Davies / Crossing A Field   62
Geraldine C. Little / Mama Out Of Donegal   63
Julia Sovrin / My Mother Speaking, In Her Age   64
Ann Goldsmith / Spring On The Frontier   65
Juanita Tobin / Last Words   66
Justine Buisson / Buttons 67
Jeanne Elliott / Buy The Large Size   69
Jean Hollander / End Of Memory   70
Leona Mahler-Sussman / Bless The Pebble On The Road   71
Alice Wirth Gray / Child In Flight   72

Charlotte Alexander / Somewhere In Erie, Pennsylvania   73
Francine Ringold / My Mother   74
Janice Thaddeus / Wedding Feast In The Forest
                              Of Compiègne   75
Paula A. Roy / Passage   76
Helen Norris / Waking   77
Harriett Susskind / In A Wheat Field Mapped Like Kansas   78
Mildred Cousens / The Egrets   79
Kaela Petrov-Levine / *Shevuos* on Campus   80
Natalie Nelson / Fire Kites   81
Maud Marshall / Elegy   82
Coco Gordon / After 41 Years, I Find A Window In My Table:
                              It Gives Me Courage   83
Geraldine C. Little / Illuminations: Fish   85
Harriett Susskind / The Lesson Of The Phoenician   85
Anneliese Wagner / Painter   87
Carol R. Hackenbruch / War Games   89
Jill Breckenridge Haldeman / Transmutations   90
Janice Thaddeus / The Voyage Out   91
Norma Westwood / The Farm: Blue Morning Light   93
Patricia Hooper / Deer In The Open Field   94
Phyllis K. Collier / Board By Board   97

Notes   98

Cover / Coco Gordon

Introduction

> *Women are the custodians*
> *of our emotional history.*
>
> Colette Inez

More than midwife, less than mother, sometimes an editor holds a newly gathered book in her hands with recognition and utter surprise. The poems in this anthology arrived through the filter of a contest designed to seek out and therefore, ratify, new poetry by mature women. The Eileen W. Barnes Award, named as a memorial to the woman whose unstipulated bequest has made this literary event possible, was offered in open competition for a book-length manuscript by a woman over forty years of age who had not yet published a book of poetry. The contest rules requested five sample poems; an editorial board of three poet-judges invited the most promising entrants to submit the complete collection; six of these manuscripts were submitted to special guest judge Colette Inez for final choice. The winning collection, *The Music of What Happens* by Ghita Orth, has now been published by Saturday Press.

Especially I wish to thank the dedicated and sensitive poets who agreed to work with me on this project which turned out to be overwhelmingly successful in reaching a wealth of women's poetry: Colette Inez, and my colleagues on the editorial board, Maxine Silverman and Rachel Hadas. Over three hundred sets of sample poems were received; thirty-two full-length manuscripts were invited for consideration. To avoid arbitrary decisions of personal taste, each of the three members of the screening board read and rated every entry before meeting to confer and vote upon the poems to be chosen.

As contestants' poems and letters from every region of the United States began pouring into the post office box, the idea of *Saturday's Women* came into being as a way of gathering some of this rich and moving expression by women who were serious poets new to literature but not to life itself. Maxine, Rachel and I found ourselves part of a community of women who were achieving evolutionary changes of the self. In the quiet of their separate girlhoods, educations, marriages, vocations, they bore the imprints of political realities. Their poems enact our most recent decades with a truth not given by newsreels where cameras tilt upward to conveyor-belt treads of tanks, or downward for crowd images of soldiers-and-sweethearts at departing trains. War, the Depression, the media—the physical and moral exigencies of our times can be felt as they *occur* in the bodies and minds of these women poets.

This anthology includes at least one poem chosen from each invited full-length manuscript, as well as some entrants' sample poems selected because they stayed with us. We have looked for poetry, not polemic. Each poem has been chosen for its own distinction; and yet, their arrangement in one volume has come about through an editing process analogous to that of cinema's. Because an individual image carries resonance from the one preceding and to the one that follows, a composition has been created in this volume. The book begins with a poem in process of "storing women." Poem by poem, we enter each new consciousness, until the last poem offers two women building together upon the "trillion waves," and the circle completes and renews itself.

Setting up this contest has been, in part, a personal search for vindication. A quarter-century of my life elapsed between the writing of my first poem (at eight) and my second. Wondering at a condition of muteness that now would be intolerable, I admit the chief reason seems to be simply that no one ever asked me to write. What were the expectations? "A girl has to get a husband by eighteen," my mother instructed, "after that, she loses her looks." Saved, I made the deadline. Where did I go? .... Into the house.... What did I do? .... Nothing to write poems about. From what had I been saved? This: responsibility for the power of words.

It took courage to emigrate from the nursery, to become a naturalized citizen in the country of myself. Even now, my first drafts may stammer with guilt, for beyond habituated landmarks of acquiescence, looms a threat of permanent exile. The freezing garret stereotype of the poet persists because of its metaphorical relevance: the artist works alone. The fortunate, however, have a literary community of peers with whom they browse in a storehouse of tradition, interconnect and kindle ideas. The isolation of the housewife in her presumably protective shroud of dependence robs her of creative signals. Expert at internalizing society's monitors, a woman must sort out her own language from a burr of exhortations.

Saturday's Women take us into intimacies of socialization that each had absorbed alone. Reliving a child-self, the poets frame such knowledge as first consciousness of sin; the terror of bleak farm winters; ABC's in German—and understand that the shape of past enthralls the present. Because women feed others spoonful by spoonful, they know that hunger is unfailing in its recurrence, that the life of a child depends utterly upon the next moment. Aware of the relentless progressions of loss, they replenish with identities of women of the past—every spring is a new frontier, new life swelling the winter skirt. Small mundane acts hold us together: a dying child is taken to the zoo; washing a dress becomes a ritual of mourning; snapping beans and the taking in of milk transform into acts of communion.

Each of the two thousand poems that came to us may be read as a separately signed declaration of poetic right. These new poets are not searching for identity so much as they are stretching themselves within the identities they are willing to confront. They are handling events with new skills at coordinating perceptions with words. They seize the days gently, turning them over like stones in water, knowing the hard or sliding textures, the glints of never-settling reflections. Their tools are fingertips, blood rhythms, and wise humor. Younger poets examine themselves as they have been cared for and hurt by others; these poets deal with the knowledge that they, too, have been those who nurture and wound. In their poems pulses the dynamic flow between pure sensory consciousness and the speaking witness. This book presents sixty-eight poems sifted from the thousands. Their voices tell us who we are and where we live.

                                        Charlotte Mandel
                                        May 4, 1982

Sheila Cowing

SUSTENANCE

It begins as soon as I come.
Your striped sweater box spills
clippings, photographs, crumbly recipes
in your writing sixty years ago
when you still unwrapped each morning
like new crystal. Now I store
while you let go:

filled cookies Aunt Clara
made on birthdays—
lard, muscats, a little lemon...

Grandma Conkie smiling
on the sand at Harborview
in the feathered hat she was embarrassed
even to have wanted...

I am storing women.
These words we keep,
these faces under egret-feathered hats
are letters from the mornings
of women: I hunger

for their news. Later I will fill
the things that go from hand to hand—
the brown glass pitcher, the bowl
I'll give to Julie when she moves.
Now I want to taste
what we season with our savings,
what we have together, this feast.

Patricia Hooper

MILK

You wake early one morning,
hear the milk being settled again between door and screen,
hear the truck leaving,
and go down in bare feet, taking the milk
into the house, to hear, as you enter the kitchen,
those voices back from the grave: your father and mother
pouring the milk from the clear pitcher, its whiteness
the pure whiteness of winter. Nothing is missing:
your cat, the sun on the table, the smell of oilcloth,
and the school bus arriving at last on the gravel road.
As you drink, you can taste them, the rich mornings
                                        of childhood
cold in your throat, reliable, filling the spaces
of a dawn thinner than breath.

Sandra Demarest

RUNNING AWAY

Months later there will be a card
A picture of a bay-mare pulling a trolley
While women in large hats smile
In the green, watered light.
It is warm here. Kiss Brother for me. Love.

This morning Lily, holding the baby,
Stands dumb with wonder on the back porch
While her mother escapes through the kitchen garden
Across the ruptured fields toward Hopewell
And the railroad station.

From the chestnuts in the sideyard
A dove begins to cry
Then the unmilked cow, the baby,
And all six children.
The great vowel sound rolls
Toward the woman, but she puts her hands
Over her ears and starts to run.

The father returns from Staunton the next day
With a new pig to kill, and packets of butterbeans
And seed corn. He sees her kitchen—
Milk clabbered. Her soap in the sink
Gone back to lye and jasmine.
Dried beans, spilled by the window,
Drank rain all night and lie astonished
Each with a white foot through the belly.

That night the train stops near Fayetteville
For water, and she steps down from the lighted coach.
She stands for a moment, stars held
To her forehead like ice;
The voices of her children rattle on her ribs.
From the pinewoods there comes a first
Tar smell of Spring.

Phyllis K. Collier

TRAPPING GOPHERS

Sometimes we would start early before the slow
August sun began its itinerary, leaving
its hot refuse over the white grass. I would wait
for him on the porch, my skin swimming. Bees
would rise, punctuating the hollyhocks and peonies
growing along the matrix of yellow pickets
warbling down the lawn.

We would climb into the car, each with our own
private certainties, my father's tan gleaming as bullion
behind his cigar, the smoke rising like praise.
It was a '36 Plymouth painted green with a brush.
Hand-painted herons splayed themselves, stiff-legged
and arrogant, the sign on the doors saying *Herron Bros.
Pest Control.* The Plymouth would crawl like a plump amphibian

over Tulsa. An arsenal of cans and gallon jugs crouched
in the back floorboards, my father's chemicals raising
their insistent questions. Heat after summer
heat he would carefully fold their names
over and over into my mind, like love.
Pyrethrum. carbon bisulfide. sulfuric acid. cyanide.
Their plain realities danced past the paleness

of summers, their mysteries pleasing
my father. Then I could not think *my private lessons.
Mercury. Venus. Earth. Mars,* he would repeat. *Order
from the sun, daughter. Do you know them now?
Jupiter. Saturn. Uranus.* I dreamt their cool masses
in a sky dark as closets. My father would clamp
his Roi Tan, purring, his eyes turned slivers of his lights.

Chlordane would sting the floor, its carpet worn to strings.
We dug holes clean as hollow logs in the furious
green of the lawns, the wings of his fingers gentle
as swans, allowing so much, throwing in the glorious
matchflames. Sometimes we would lay traps
he had made himself, the wood and old springs
poised at the edge of the holes like predators.

At noon, our turtle-car would dawdle
and wheeze, smelling like old eggs,
to the Silver Castle on Peoria Street
where hamburgers big as faces hissed on the grill.
Across the street at Monty's Parlour,
cool as catfish,
my father would lunch on 3.2 Muhlbach, his acids

lurking in the car. The windows in the Plymouth rolled down
and yawning in the heat, we would float
past the sycamore trees, the sun flashing messages
to the gracious lawns mowed and lovely over their gophers
starting to burrow again. Going back,
my father would mull his cigar, listening to the blue
thief of his atmosphere stealing his breath.

Patricia Dobler

THEIR MARRIAGE/MEMORY

Their voices still wake me
as I woke for years to that rise and fall,
the rope pulled taut between them,

both afraid to break or let go.
Years spilled on the kitchen table,
picked over like beans or old bills.

What he owed to the mill, what she wanted
for him. Tears swallowed and hidden
under layers of paint, under linoleum rugs,

new piled on old, each year the pattern
brighter, costlier. *The kids*
he would say, *if it weren't for*

She'd hush him and promise
to smile, saying *This is what
I want, this is all I ever wanted.*

Shelley Ehrlich

JOB'S WIFE

> *Then said his wife unto him: "Dost thou still hold fast thine integrity? blaspheme God, and die."*
> Job 2:9

    1

This has become his story,
but call her by her name. Let
it be Dina, Molly,
Suzanne. Know she was blood
and flesh, a woman observing
dew, flights of birds,
the tidal drain of coves
and surging in of fish. Recall

the events. Not one, but all
her children killed, the house
and fields destroyed, Job with
unremitting boils and only
words of praise. Before you say:
each of us is Job, pause
a moment with that partial

truth. Think of trails hiked
in Job's mountains. Lost to comrades,
blinded, aged by snow, you probed
a wilderness, felt the chill
factor overcome the banked
fires of your blood. But then,
the hut signalled. Disaster begins
when pain becomes ordinary
and durable, like the trowel
we dig the garden with. Do you

suppose in the only words she spoke
she missed the possibility of *bless,*
missed how silver flashes
when wind whips the hemlock?
Her children dead, Job burning in
his marrow, she chanced what other

women chance: hedged in her love,
chose words and struck
the silent temple of his grief.

2

I call her Dina. She
inhabits my house. Often
when I breathe I hear
her inhale. From room

to room, she intuits
my tasks. To water plants,
pluck dead leaves, bring
in mail, slice tomatoes
into wheels. What rites

must I perform to keep
her here? She crossed
the swinging bridge I
built, secured with string
wound in a drawer of used-up
things. History reveals

her public griefs. How walls
cracked, rain clogged
her shoes, beetles crawled
into the gardens and all
the petals dropped.

But what of private
griefs? How she stood beside
Job, his flesh on fire. Did
her skin burn, her tongue
thicken? Now I want to hear

her speak, record how she
tilts her head, leans across
the table to help me
snap the beans.

Ghita Orth

ELEPHANTS—A MYTHOLOGY

Your quick childhood
was trumpeted by elephants—
a tuskless one, calicoed
red and white, hugged into bursting,
leaking its plastic cells
like seeds into your hair;
small grey models ranked staunchly
on your shelf, Indian, African,
their fat knees wrinkled by the carver's hand
over unbending joints; and the elephant
of seamless words I made for you
when you were made to lie, unmoving,
on the steel table in the steel room
under a red-flowering machine eye.

Microphoned through deaf, lead walls,
Edgar the Elephant, galumphing loose
in Central Park, smiled shyly
under his trunk and stroked the backs
of small boys just like you,
saying *lie still, lie still.*
Then after the room unclenched
we rode the crosstown bus
to Zoo elephants, slit-eyed and real,
who pointed soft hairy mouths
at the peanuts slipping from your lax hand.

When you begged elephant drawings
from the doctor charting your disappearance
with his blunt pen,
when you marched elephants
heavy-footed through your imaginings,
was it so you might see
calves holding tight
to their parents' rope-tough tails,
trunks twined fast to such bulking safety
that you could dream of never letting go
or getting lost?

Carol R. Hackenbruch

FAR FROM THE LAKE WITHOUT FOGHORN

Walking this road through trees,
I push fog against current.
Two deer jump, scatter pebbles and sand,
span ditch and shrubs.

Their footprints fill with fog;
I search the cuts for direction,
a charm of sorts,
a way beyond gravel
rearranged with each step.

Kneeling,
I see Trillium
just out of reach,
faded to lavender of its middle age.

Unsure of moss
on the north or south of a tree,
marooned on this road
without a sound to guide,
I hold my own hand,
lavender darkening.

Mary Kay Rummel

HOW ONE LEAVES THE ORDER

1 *The Fantasy*

It is the face
of water. One side
a still blue eye
the other a gray
thrashing.
Behind it all the swamp
where birches lose
their slim images.

When I look
into water I see
my own face smooth
then broken again and again.
When I look
into it I fall
my own shattered eyes
mending.

I lived once
in the swamp
tangled in roots
I had little knowing of
explored that cloistered world
swam dark corridors
looking for long sealed doors
forced my eyes to stay open long
after they wanted to close.
Now it is the deep lake
clear and wild
that I love.

2 *The Ceremony*

It happens in a boat on Whitefish Lake
as you and the loons watch the day end.

Beneath you the blue grey belly
of yesterday's rain.

You watch as if your life did not depend
on it. Watch as the sun screams from its isolated
point. It moves through spasms of color until
a blue veil carries it away. The loons wear
the straightness of night on their heads. They want
to fill it with their cries.

Then you know you carry your own grief. The cries
you hear in the night are yours. And he
will never be grief to you again.

3   *The Decision*

it is flowing
down a river
that twists and slides
shadow into sunlight
into shadow

snag a rock
hesitate
then shove off again
hills and undersides of leaves
sway in the lean
and clouded light I float in
the currents
of my choice

summers
night in the north country
comes late
there is a silence
borne in the bodies
of trees that hover between

two worlds long
as if they could choose
which to be in

I too hang
on that edge knowing
it is unnecessary
I carry my own night

4 *The Falling Back*

Just when you figured you could do it
walk off the dock into clear water
get your hair wet say it straight out
you get caught again on the corner
of a word aimed at the heart and you begin
to struggle again.

Just when you figured you had it in you
the hard part that you could carry away
you find that isn't really it at all
even here by the long limbed lake
it isn't the walking away that counts
it's the freedom to do it.

You are so wounded by his silence. Arrow
in the chest missing the heart. Vital
organs are fine but there is danger
of infection. You just walk around
with it sticking out of both sides until someone
gets near enough to pull it out.

5 *The Feeling That You Carry It With You*

You are so wounded by that silence.
Be like the loons who play wounded on the water

who rise up with high pitched screams and fall
floating black humps in the vast lake.

But it is all for distraction a pretense.

> Come take them
> Can't you see they are weak
> follow them in a wide course
> over the moon water
> then watch them shoot suddenly
> upward their bodies their cries
> black northbound arrows
> across the sunset

Wounds that are no wounds.

6 *Morning*

Down a dirt road
to the round onyx swamps
where birches preen
and a wild canary flashes
its cry is newborn surprising
a gift to this hour of the wild raspberry.

Sheila Cowing

THE HINGE

Down on the beach we separate,
you to the sun and the morning *Times,*
I to the tidal pools and the casual
treasure last night's wind and rain washed in.
Beneath my toes the mud and the hard rounded shells.

We've been paired like the valves of these mollusks
for more than twenty years now, held
by the strong adductor muscles of children
and the old decencies. Mostly we've liked
the bond.
                Its toothed hinge, clean
of detritus, the shell can strain food
through its single siphon. We let it open
and close. Once a friend suggested
we'd been lucky. I flared—it wasn't luck,
it was hard work. It wasn't, not really,

not like digging clams or preparing a fine
bouillabaisse. Grit, weed, algae—all flow in
with the tide and out, even sewage
which, like crisis, urges growing.
Oh things slip in and rankle,

a dear attractive friend wanting
too much solace, one dreary meal too many.
But it's when something rigid,
this guilt, a sliver wedged
in the hinge, fails to wash out in new tide,

then—then the breach—and the slow
relentless drying. To survive the daily
low tide becomes hard work.

Anneliese Wagner

OUR STORIES

I twist tongue
lick ABCs from honeycomb
above the blackboard
while savage numbers
giggle in a row

We heathens
speak no English
eins Anneliese
zwei Mutti and Papa
in their bed
drei I snuggle in

Vier in my village yard
laced into new patent shoes
I stick to the kitchen step
until Mutti spreads paper
over the chickshit cobbles
until bang! an oven door
slams my house down

At P.S. Atlantis,
The Bronx
"A" loops Anneliese until
you're in America now
floats a black swan
off the doublefold

Rabbit foot "Anna"
charms me from digits
across my forearm
from count   division
from zero   minus
freeze   mother   eyes

from names without letters
and bone chip numbers
that flake on windy days
off ashpits
from tallow kin
your stories

Coco Gordon

FATHER THAT YOU HAVEN'T BEEN MINE,

they've covered your eyes
taken the strap and knife
away
and wood, hand-lathe, your hands, hand-wood.

Is two months too quiet?
For you have been warned to keep quiet.
No turning out wood vase, rook, gnome,
or solids oiled and wanting to be held.

A temporary blindness, but more
the turn of your head metered,
for they must keep the clouds off your eyes
as the world does its turning.

Your son told me of your organ keys.
The air would rise daily like your wife's bread
and settle on his tongue, this gentle son
who kept between the step and soul of your feet
and can repeat how effectively you kept moving.

He tells me now he can't imagine your eyes closed off.
With hands as wrested, they've reduced you to a
portrait of the planked and stiffened gothic,
fork nailed to the wall, photo in a book,
speechless, held in place.

Father that you haven't been mine, at dawn
I squirm into the page on the light side
of the sash
where by sheen of February ice
I draw pictures of sun flotation,
warm risings of dough, the eyes
of your wife loving your children.
I draw on the inside of the
sash that binds your eyes
and they are becoming green and watery,

over the black and white reduction,
over the wintered,
forcing those blanks.

Even the raucous colors of fruits and vegetables
of your labors I fill in for you to see.
Up here where it reflects in the forgotten
but ready to detonate corner
of your obediently waiting brain.

Susan Donnelly

EVE NAMES THE ANIMALS

To me, *lion* was sun on a wing
over the garden. *Dove,*
a burrowing, blind creature.

I swear that man
never knew animals. Words
he lined up according to size,

while elephants slipped flat-eyed
through water

and trout
hurtled from the underbrush, tusked
and ready for battle.

The name he gave me stuck
me to him. He did it to comfort me,
for not being first.

Mornings, while he slept,
I got away. Pickerel
hopped on the branches above me.
Only spider accompanied me,

nosing everywhere,
running up to lick my hand.

Poor finch. I suppose I was
woe to him—

the way he'd come looking for me,
not wanting either of us
to be ever alone.

But to myself I was
palomino
          raven
                  fox ...

I strung words
by their stems and wore them
as garlands on my long walks.

The next day
I'd find them withered.

I liked change.

June Rachuy Brindel

THE POET'S DAIMON

Said, *Open up, relax, you're beautiful,*
Let me hold you, there, there,
Feel that, isn't that something?
I love you, you know? See

What pleasure there is in simply
Opening up, relaxing, feeling:
You're great, you know it?
You've got what it takes, everything.

Let me in now, let me have this chance
To mix with the future. C'mon, breathe
For me, breed for me, take me, take me
With you into the generations to come.

And she was ready for it, dreaming into time
Coming, poised to wash with him through
The flood gates holding back the future—
When he softened, wilted, vanished

A long soft wail dying away with him
Over empty plains baking into desert
Hardening into moon crust, and the blank
Air shuddered with anger, and the rocks

Rose up like dams. Then
He came back. Said, *You*
Shrank from me. Why did you do that?
Don't you know and don't you know?

She did not know what he was talking about,
She had thought it was going along well.
Perhaps it was the noise that had done it,
The voices in the next room (he wanted a

Private thing), or the alarm clock and the
Feet rushing through the halls, and the squeal
Of the teakettle, all those mouths waiting
To be fed, and the dust falling

And the children scratching at the door,
Pulling at the sheets, and the typing
Piled up, and the posing to be done,
The bright lights congealing her sight.

I can't see behind the bulbs,
She explained. *I don't
Have time to think.*
And he was gone again.

Virgins dry (he let it be known)
Into venomous spinners, snatching lovers
From anywhere, draining them into husks
And still thirsty in an endless drought.

They are shells rattling against driftwood, sucked
Into dark funnels trailing over cracked river beds.
(He sucked his pipe.) They are a howl of sand
Tearing at deserted boathouses, parchment skin (he howled).

Now, in this late hour, in the aging silence,
She hears him again at her door.
He whispers, *Let me in now, there is still time!
C'mon, breed for me. Take me. Take me with you.*

31

Norma Westwood

SEATED, THE BODY FEELS AS IF

it sticks up too far, or at
an odd angle above its horizon
of hips. Where in space
does it belong, and why?
Resting next to me, his hands,
having decided not to move
again, have the fierce pathos
of the dumb. Speech is a hammering
of iron into nails. It takes
all day and nothing
has ever been written down.
This is why the beggar child,
crippled by its parents,
accepts all without question
or philosophy—it has never
heard the word cruelty.
It believes in limbs that drag
like flippers over the earth,
scraping open.

Caroline Knox

THE CRYBABY AT THE LIBRARY

There was a crybaby at the library.
Tears were pouring heavily down his face.
He had omitted to do his math
and thought of the anger of his teacher
as the tears fell on his knitted
mittens between the fingers and thumb.

It is raining all over inside the library.
Parts of the brick walls are curling up
and plaster is falling on the heads and beards of students.
It is very dangerous for the books.
The rain comes down from every beam
and the professors do not know whether they should wrap
their articles in themselves or themselves in their articles.
The beautiful new botany professor who is only twenty-six
    and has marvelous dark eyes
has makeup running down her face as she runs out the door.

A precious incunabulum inside a glass case
is swimming gently as if in a dishpan.
Tiny letters and pieces of gold that were put there in 1426
are lifting off and turning into scum.
The assistant librarians are afraid to use the telephones
because yellow sparks are coming out of them.
Several young men go up to the attic, saying that the trouble
    may be from up there.
The electricity goes off and people are standing
between the floors in dangerously wet elevators.
The librarians' kleenex and aspirin are wet and are melting
    into each other in the desk drawers.
The Shakespeare professors come out of the Shakespeare Room
and look around and go back in again; they must stay with
    the ship.
Fog is rising like rugs between the bookstacks
People are laughing in a brittle way to disguise their
    well-grounded panic.

The botany professor is a redemptive figure.
She goes to the Maintenance Department and reports what
 is happening in the library.
Eventually the Maintenance Department goes over and
 fixes things.
The crybaby is definitely *not* a redemptive figure—he sits
still self-absorbed and shivery, and crying and crying,
and not at all trying to catch up on his math, nor even trying
 to fake it,
and all the time waves of water dash over his Bean boots
and up onto his lap, splashing his notebooks.
For the impending disgust of his teacher is foremost in his mind
as tears are foremost on his cheeks, where he sits crying and
 crying in the library.

Elaine Dallman

MARIA BONNIFEMME DIED IN 1672

Her aunt used to say Maria glided her tongue across stone walls.
She needed coolness. She was five.

Moving within her cloistering family,
like gliding behind a gauze screen, she (or someone)
poisons that aunt, two uncles, one brother younger than she.

An adolescent, she visits the hospital;
the softness of small firm breasts,
her saint-like thinness, are noted.
Four patients die.

The black frocked men of the town
know Maria is the betrayer, know
Burning
roots out that which terrifies women and men.
They sign this statement.

Then they watch the movement
to the right, to the left, of fIre.
Trance-watching is burning her to nakedness.
They watch the fire's play with the blistering skin.

In 1676, protecting themselves with toads, people
dig in the wheat fields away from the town,
to find her bones.

She has given proof: the poisonings continued.

They take the charred bones.
They place the relic bones before faces of plaster
in front of the altars.
They genuflect. They ignite incense.
They kneel in prayer.

Katherine Wells

ASK THE CHILD ABOUT RELIGION

Seven summers
in the cauldron of Kansas,
nothing breaks like this.
My sins are immense.

It is August.
Farm women sweat
in cotton print dresses
assured of salvation.

I wad my handkerchief
with a dime tied in the corner
saved for the collection plate.

My knees are ridged
from kneeling
on hard oak boards
while all the elders pray.

Page one hundred of the hymnal,
Let the water and the blood,
Mrs. Orgus, old and deaf,
drones a different verse

and agitates a fan
imprinted with psalms
and a picture of Hansen's
funeral home.

The preacher's voice
rises and falls like an ax.
I boil in my guilt.

Damnation is everywhere
as Jesus recedes
like a wave.

I am small
and incapable
of heaven.

Ann Woolfolk

TWISTER

A friend driving south through Virginia,
saw the S&H Feed Store
lifted off its foundations by a tornado
and dropped nearby,
grain dripping from little windows.
This is how a mental breakdown begins.
Disaster curls closer with its little warnings.
The synapses overload with a cruel energy.
You can hardly stand still.
When suddenly, lifted far above
all that is comfortable and clear,
you see the earth, the egg it is,
grow small, combust and disappear.
You hear your mother's voice, calm and sad,
calling you in from the street.
And you think you are home, home at last,
until you are set down hard,
close to where you took off,
cracked and injured.

Barbara Ewell

RIVERVIEW HOTEL FOR WOMEN

1 *Mrs. Haney*

I am too old for three flights up, but what's
A woman to do? It's cheap. Cheap. Across
The street trains bang in the night, their coupling guts
Spill into my sleep, their sound a sauce
For rancid meat. My life is this. Ceiling
To floor, walled up with books and photographs
In boxes never undone, congealing
In this unforgiving heat. My son laughs
From his leather frame, his hair like dry straw
Blown over his smooth head. I hear the lock
On Mag's thin door, bolt checked three times. I saw
That student sneak in with a boy. They'll be
At it all night. It's cheap. It galls me sour
To be like this, to hear the moans that he
Gives her. To live like this, with no set hour
To rise. Out of habit, I wind the clock,
Make the bed, dust the chair, chest and phone.
Its book holds what's left of my husband's name.
I trace the print. Touch it like braille. Alone.
Hear them? Disgusting. They don't know a shame
In this world. I hate that kid. It's not right
To be old and cramped and sickened by fright.

2 *Mag*

I lock my door
turn around twice
lock my door again
I sit on the bed
smile real nice
give me a gulp of gin

Fly away devil
fly away spook
the dead take a snooze with no shoes on

Go away cowboy
go away gook
eat your supper while the news is on

Beth has a boy
or the boy's got her
so lock the door again
shopping bag spilled
its goods last week
better to sleep with gin

Come near angel
come near ghost
the bed goes squeakidy-squeak
holy mum Mary
pity thou child
most frail and drunk and meek

That girl's hair's like
a duckling's down
wonder if she'd like some gin
her boy's skin's mahogany brown
guess I better not go in

Go to sleep Margaret
go to sleep girl
the world has enough of pain
brown and gold
make an ox-eye swirl
Mary bless loving insane

3 *Beth*

I sleep
under flaying plaster
with duckbill shapes
and dolphin-tailed silhouettes

in a space where nothing grand can be done

nothing grand is ever done
in a space or a time
grand is a child's slinky toy
down tenement steps
spreading rumors to a neat heap

the old widow next door
holds anger
like a fat woman her purse
on the Front Street bus

I will not be old
that way

the drunk lady across the hall
shuffles in terry slides
in winter she wears several socks,
one sweater, two caps
her shopping bag holds these now

see that shadow
by the transom?
what does it look like to you?
no...
I didn't think of that
to me?
an ear of corn
all mummy wrapped
growing from bedrock
gold energy piercing its side

kind of a christ at age 12

that's all right
I don't understand either
sometimes I just see things
once I saw Sancho with Jesus

I think it was Jesus

Anne Harter-Jones

WHY DO THEY KEEP A CANARY

While I was there her bird died.
Sitting in her bright spring kitchen
she was baking an improvised apple
pastry with old apples that she
said were no good. I
was the only one who ate any, &
to me it was wonderful. She consumed
only cigarettes & saccharine coffee &
said at 100 lbs she still feels fat.

While I was there her bird died.
I came to distract her while she
waited for the hospital to call
her in & the sounds of her small house
were strange to me, *What is that hum?*
I asked, it was the electric clock
& that sound like burning paper?
I looked, it was the bird shuffling
around on the floor of its cage.
Why doesn't it sit on its perch?
I asked. Its leg was paralyzed
from a stroke. She read me some old
anger & some old love &
told me some old beauty
& I marveled how she could recall
the names of all the Michigan
wildflowers. *90% of me
is entirely sane,* she said.

While I was there her bird died.
I read her some new anger
& some new cynicism but no new love &
she said it was so sophisticated
& together we consumed cigarette
after cigarette & many large
children came in & did not eat her
apple pastry, but ate Banquet
pot pies & there was no more

rustling like fire from the bottom
of the cage & no one minded
that the bird had died. A child
buried it in the backyard & she
said, *Wash your hands before
you eat the pot pie.* I was
finishing up her husband's bottle
of Dry Sack sherry & we both smoked.

While I was there her bird died.
The little house was full of big
children consuming pot pies instead
of apple pastry & not caring
whether the bird had died &
the hospital didn't call & I
wouldn't leave until the sherry
was all gone & the 90% of her
that was completely sane told me
beautiful and articulate things.
I wondered how much of me
was wholly sane, but didn't
mention it because I was there
as a distraction & suspected
I couldn't separate my sanity
into percentages & better not try.
I finally left when there was
no more sherry & she wanted to
leave, but the hospital hadn't called.

While I was there her bird died.
Why do they keep a canary
in the bottom of a mine shaft?

LoVerne Brown

REMATCH

Lady in the polkadot dress
in what century
did we claw each other bloody
for man or ruby?
Meeting now, your recognition is instant;
your nails pop into position
red and ready
your eyes compute my reach
you slide into stance like a pro...

O.K., I accept your challenge—
we'll square off by the pool—
I'll bleed if I have to.
But first—forgive my amnesia—
there are things I need to be told:

Was the man flawless
or the ruby clean-cut?
Are you left or right handed?

Francine Ringold

HOW WAS I TO KNOW

for Lisa

how was i to know
that the woman sitting next to me
was a crow
her hair shining
and black and her eyes
beads of black in almond pools
i should have seen
the circle of five orange seeds
placed in front of her
cross-legged on the grass
but she was silent

covered with a dust rose shawl
thin wire rings in her ears
feet bound in chinese slippers
nails painted vermilion
lips gold lustre
her breast flat
next to me
beating
hidden under a dust shawl
she
waiting
to eat
each kernel
of corn
growing on my land

Lisa Ress

GRANDMOTHER'S HOUSE: THE BABA YAGA

Yellow claws start from the pot,
blue chicken thighs are rigid on the plate.
She is sucking soup and chewing carefully.
Carp eyes in gelatin, glazed scales.
From the glassfront cabinet, my grandpa,
soft and hungry, stares.

I am six, I am eight, I am ten.
I am her juicy dove, her little eel and pigeon pie.

Inside the bed's white throat, my legs
lie stiff against the sheet.
All night she is brushing out her hair, stretching it.
Brushing out her hair, brushing mine,
winding the hanks on narrow spools.

Roberta Chester

HEARTWOOD

You can tell nothing from a man's heart
if you lay it on the table,
except that it is thick and hard
and veined and has flaps
that open either way.
But nothing about the way it beats
and the chemistry of its blood
could tell you where it was going
or where it's been,
could tell you what that man would do
if you reached out to him
because something hurt,
or whether it ever stopped still
for the sound of a voice
or a tree—

It's different with a piece of wood.
Cut in lengths and lying on a heap of logs
you can tell from the heart of it—
whether it came from a maple or a beech,
how high it reached,
how it stood against the wind,
the shape and color of the leaves
when the tree was full of flames.
You could tell from the start
when that piece of wood comes off the saw,
how it will burn
how long it will keep you warm—
you can tell about the stuff
that lingers on
when the fire is out—
the texture of the ash,
the measure of the creosote.

Ruth F. Eisenberg

SOME THINGS YOU CAN'T FORGET

for Saul N.

How tossing the baby in the air
for target practice
they filled it full of holes
flipped it back to the mother
How mocking they
ordered the line of march
not counting
on living witnesses

At our kitchen table you
pried your words, reluctant rocks
from a buried past
We studied our knuckles
heard the refrigerator stop humming
the dripping tap loud as a tattoo

Jean Hollander

A JOURNALIST INTERVIEWS TWO WOMEN IN CAMBODIA

We enter the world
    through narrow gates
        and gather new flesh

        brief was our joy
            an iridescence crouched
                over maidenheads

            with the fragrance of children
                we were rewarded
                    for stench of birth

                    growing they grew our hurt

now our huts are silent—
    why light a fire
        to warm one cup?

        like a nagging tree limb
            our sagging breasts
                dropped their weight at last

            in the radiant fields
                our bones go about their task
                    bending from plant to plant

                    with slower tenderness

we have rehearsed
    positions of mourning
        into a dance

    we have given
        our men and daughters
            to the diving hawk

            under the leafless mimosa
                we scattered
                    their familiar shreds

                    to droughty earth

the sky need not water
    nor dust deliver green
        when hearts of men are ashened

        like a widow's head:
            denial devours
                even hunger and grief

                young man, do not trouble
                    how we shall live—
                        when our stores are eaten

                        we will eat less

Ann Z. Leventhal

SNAPSHOT

It's sand, *the woman's saying.* I took it
near Danang, Pleiku, or some other place
that was levelled. In those days
I was an Army Nurse,
but this is the picture
that sticks. It's of the God
damned grit that

shifted between my teeth,
clogged my throat, I couldn't
speak, had to empty
socks, eyes, ears, then pretend
I could brush the crap off
sheets issued us our first day over there,
sheets already spotted with blood. As if

sand like this here isn't bad
enough, those drifts leaning
against barracks walls, fences,
sand waiting for choppers
to whip up the action, set the place
cracking, sand tearing into the backs
we turned, the eyes we shut

so no one, in those stinging twisters
could make out the dark Vietnamese
stares polished bright by the horror
that was us. Even now some can't name the game
we lost—dominoes or maybe body counts. Today
they talk about first strikes, that's playing
for keeps which is why I keep showing this

though I know it's amateurish, only an Instamatic
print more than ten years old, and awful
smudged. Still, doesn't this picture
make one point perfectly clear?
It's not just
them but us too buried under
that sand. Can you see?

Ellin Carter

TWO-DIMENSIONAL RECALL

Picture Nelson and Jeanette
remaking *Star Wars:* no alien
visage approximating
her mask, his space suit
bulging like the Mountie uniform
in *Rose Marie.* Everything
else, flatland.

I'd like to think I sat through
three straight shows of *Maytime*
to see Nelson get it in the end,
to hear Jeanette finally crack,
treacle (*will you remember?*)
trickle from those violet eyelids,
butterscotch dribble into silence,
destroyed. In truth, I had succumbed,
in stardust reverie, to dark
stirrings, smouldering in
celluloid.

My best friend and I had genuine
Nelson Eddy, Jeanette MacDonald
paper dolls, with all the costumes.
Though we broke tabs, lost parasols,
and could not make limbs come apart,
the paper slid (*ah, sweet mystery!*)
one flat surface pressed upon another,
vibrating purple and orange.

Please don't scorn those games.
They taught us all we needed
to know of life, they
and the silver screen. And
the junior high lecturer
who said, "Girls, it is time
for you to start wearing
girdles. They will hold you in."

Phebe Hanson

STURDY ARMS

You've got sturdy arms,
he said to me,
my blind date
back in 1947,
a Norwegian student
studying
to be a missionary
to Madagascar.
You'd make a good worker
out on the mission field.
I stood on the steps
of Sivertsen Hall,
Augsburg College—
a few feet below me
the Mississippi River
moved past
to the university.
That's where I should've gone,
I thought to myself,
where I'd meet some decent men,
atheists and agnostics
who'd be studying
to get rich someday,
let me hire cleaning women
so I could sit for hours
in my room
with my sturdy arm
moving across the page
writing poem after poem after poem.

Lois V. Walker

THE WAR CAME TO ILLINOIS

The war crawled all over us
in the spring of 1942.
It got into the family apartment
above my mother's shop by wire.
It devoured the newspapers
in huge irregular chunks.
It sprayed a heavy voice
around the local theater
where distant gray boats exploded at sea
and rivet men kept marching
to point at Hitler on his balcony.
It swallowed up familiar male faces
my friend and I had admired
downtown on Saturday nights.
It deposited khaki at a near-by army base
to cover unknown men who would come around
looking for fun, who might
need girls, we were told—
even twelve year olds, like us—
men, like the private first class
who followed us one time
until we stopped in front of my place
who motioned us to join him
around the corner where it was dark
who watched and waited while we
started to giggle, but froze instead
who stayed put and motioned again
half man, half shadow in and out of light
until a couple came to break the spell
and we ran for the front door
without looking back.
The war crawled all over us
in the spring of 1942.
It chewed the edges of everything green
and that was just the beginning.

Lisa Ress

LEARNING THE ROPES. EVANSTON, 1949

for Kathy, who always played shipwreck with me.

Showering there is more than the single showerhead.
I test myself, how long I can go without breathing.
The icy road to school is the way to the work camp.
I make it through.
The elevated is a cattle car that seals me in with strangers.
I study them. Who will be the first to crack?
Who will not look away when I have to go to the bathroom?
Sundays before our parents awake, we jump our wrecked ship,
hit the refrigerator for provisions to stock our beds.
We rescue each stuffed animal.
This time we will get away with our lives.

Elizabeth Anne Socolow

CITYSCAPE

in memoriam Gertrude Goldman

My aunt, seventy-eight, playful as a hoop
missed her 5 o'clock game of checkers
with the janitor's son, ten years old.

He wouldn't believe her absence
from the table in the backyard, went
to find her naked in ropes, in her bedroom

closet after violation by a stranger.
He released her himself, talking to her,
while he used the scissors he found in the kitchen.

When she left that apartment
with her ivory mahjong set she moved in with
her two sisters who hated games.

When I visited she spoke of the boy.
She showed me the cards he sent;
raging at the printed verse, she

kissed his signature.

Susan Donnelly

CONSTELLATION

Although the stranger dragged me from my car,
I am not robbed
of my lover's smell or touch
nor of the arch of colors
when he moves inside me.

Although I screamed up the deaf street,
my friends Betsy and Joan
laugh with me
around my kitchen table
and the jealous cat
creeps up
to warm my lap.

Although the abandoned house had doom eyes
and the graffiti mocked me,
my mother
teaches me the names of flowers,
splitting milkweed pods
so that their silver abundance
lightens the air.

Although he tore off my clothes,
Sister Theresa Mary
hands me the Latin prize.
I see dust
puff from the crimson
auditorium curtain.

Although he beat me to the ground
and that room stank
of ash and urine
and dead animals,
my grandfather calls me
Pixie.
From the back lawn after supper
he shows me
Cassiopeia
and the Hunter
who move as we move.

Although the thuds,
the panting
and pig squeals that came from me
enclosed a deep silence,
pieces of moments
tumble smooth for me
like all the mauve and brown pebbles
gathered on Nauset Beach.

Barbara Winder

RIDE UP THE MOUNTAIN

We waited in a line of panting
cars while they cleaned the glass
and oil from the road. Finally,
a tow-truck squirmed its way
through our unhappy queue, its
revolving light thin in heavy
rain. I watched your profile
against the night, your beard
strong and stern as Melville's
as he sat, contemplating
Ahab. You, tired, just having
explained your divorce, the three
handsome children, the debts.
My mind whirled like the flashers
on the cop cars; in a revolution
of red and white I saw us
whirling on this silly earth.
Then, in the sore and bleeding
night I saw the man behind us
kiss the girl beside him
as if they were in a drive-in
and the wreck now pulling past us,
smashed and doorless,
were on film.

Elizabeth Williams

THE SUNBATHERS

Over Mazatlan the sky smiles
with gold teeth. Yolanda in a hot pink bikini
is stroking her thighs with the Avon Lotion
she sells to the ladies of Sinaloa.
Leonardo, the architect, remembers a Spanish
proverb: *Los regalos ablandan corazones*
and he gives her a circle of seaweed.
Fong Choy says: *When people are dumb*
they can go to the university.
Gustavo must get back to his cattle.
Hector just sits there smiling under
the thatched roof of his sunglasses.

A horse and rider come galloping up the beach
and I think of Juanita.
Her father rode with Zapata in 1911
and she with him, stirring the soup.
Now in the wisdom of her ninety-one years
she drinks a quart of gin every night,
curses politicians on television and
gets up in the morning to diaper the baby.

> *Do you really live in this earth*
> *Not forever in this earth, only a little here.*
> *Even if it's from jade it breaks.*
> *Even if it's from gold it breaks.*
> *Even if it's turkey feathers, it's pulled out.*
> *Not forever in this earth, only a little here.*

In the museum in Mexico City
The President is blessing the exhibits
a brass band booming amplified grasshoppers.
He walks through the gulch of applause,
pausing in the stiff uniform of Presidents
grey hair, grey suit, black tie,
handsome in the manner of all politicians
in the manner of a basket of plumed snakes.
He walks turkey-breasted out into the sun
which melts him down to grey shadow
in the black limousine.

High on the rocks the white temple gleams
Moorish arches and white, white stucco
the blue water behind, less green in it,
with the hardness and boldness of mosaic.
From the sangria-stained windows
disco rhythms pound like a puny sea
                The sunbathers
dance under silver moons
under studdings of red and orange stars.

Now the moon rises out of the sea
Quetzalcoatl comes riding out of the sea
weaving a tunic of conchshell
wound in the mouth of a snail.
He comes offering a bowl of *pulque*
saying *Ich liebe dich, Jeg elsker deg*
armed with the white light of Norway.
Quetzalcoatl, it has been so long since you
gathered the bones of the dead
sprinkled them with your sperm.
What will you do with these brilliant bar flies?
How will you clear the smoke from our eyes?

Barbara Langham

AUNT MATTIE DYING

She'd been standing at the sink,
peeling potatoes,
when she said, *I don't know
what's the matter with me.
Maybe I'm dying,* and Mother
told her, *Go sit down
if you don't feel well,*
and she said, *No,
I'll be okay,*
and kept unrolling
those brown skins.

Jeanne Elliott

MY MOTHER'S POETRY CIRCLE

Mournful ballads round their meeting hours
with triolets, rondels, *terza rima*
on faded love and Time's swift course,
sestina lengths embroidered at both ends,
drooping cinquains sad as yellow leaves,
Clara, Vera, Ada and their friends.

Clara, you hurled yourself across my body,
flattened us both on rotten potato peels
in one corner of the hog wallow.
Blood ran in my mouth. I bellowed,
struck, broke your glasses,
a five-year old fury face down in slop.
But the keening funnel lifted over us,
louder than a hundred freight trains.
The chicken house exploded in feathers and shit.
For years I smelled sweat and manure in your embrace
at every Friday Grange Hall social.

Ada, hard gales flayed the prairie raw that spring.
One late March day we watched the darkness
gather in doomsday clouds beyond the cottonwoods,
noonday darkness tinged with greenish light.
Three screaming children ran for the moist shelter
of your arms. Wet feedsacks to our faces,
we huddled by the pantry's farthest onion bin.
Dust fine as flour stung our streaming eyes,
rimmed our mouths. Terror turned acid in our throats.
Your voice came steady from the whirling shadows,
"Pray through the cloth. God won't mind."

Vera, think of bleak December long ago:
a household heavy with two weeks' vigilance,
filling croup kettles beside a tented crib,
slept at last, burrowed into patchwork quilts
like freezing animals seeking their holes
while midwinter ravaged the open plains.
At midnight the base burner's red heart failed;
alone in your chair you did not waken,
and a two years' child strangled in her phlegm.
You lay a week beyond speech or moving;
Grandmother put white satin rosebuds in her hands.

The Circle writes sonnets, every foot in place,
on blighted love and springtime's ivory buds.
They plod through stark syllabic lines, spin
Spenserean stanzas rich in knightly quests,
quatrains, couplets, rime royal's easy gallop,
each image swathed in memory's distanced haze,
Clara, Ada, Vera.

Nancy Davies

CROSSING A FIELD

We're crossing a field again. It's the same
time of year: nothing green, everything
wishing to be. You are indistinguishable
from unopened leaves. Beneath your skin
swim glees of transparent fish.

Expanding sun overlays shaded
cornfields. Gold bones of last year's harvest
wake ready for burial. It remains cold,
the ground sustains us where naked
stems interlace in a woven basket.

We run; or perhaps you are floating,
an unmoored seine in the river. I follow
smiling as in my photos. Willows once more are
gilding; the gray partridge hurtles
from hiding; this happens each year.

Last spring we went south, the soil was ruddy
and potters made vases for flowers;
women hung cheese in the yards. Once I saw
in a red jar figs black as the hair of a
mandarin's lady; the jar curved like a womb.

Here in the north light differs. Two trees
on a slope construe forests, while sky
stands vertical, innocent, everywhere. This
exists as before. Discarded feathers of swans
brush our dual image onto the millpond

you never pause for. Without motion the field
strokes my ankles. Now nothing moves but the meadow
lark's flute played in the painted straw.
You must wait to help an old woman climb
over a fence. She carries eggs in a kerchief.

Geraldine C. Little

MAMA OUT OF DONEGAL

    Hands
are the center of the story.
      Nothing like moths or the Monarch
now flaming to sea on faith.
    Small, worked
        weblike over
          supple & muscle

(six children the workers of webs)

    Listen. Her world is black & white
keys, the press of pedals. London
    and a College of Music move
        fingers like firesparks. We read
reviews: England, Scotland, Ireland
    great halls glowing.

Before I was married, she thunders
Rachmaninoff, Bartok, Scriabin
    the room of her own we sit in
        silent, listening to waterfalls,
          quick-eyed birds & lizards
            daisies just coming to belief.

    It was a winter of blaze:
sunfall on frost. And the dark illness
    crept in, furnished
        her bright rooms for a long stay,
          the longer dying.

    Sometimes in firelight
I form shadow creatures with my hands.
      Nothing like hers.
          It's the webs I can't weave
that I would like to play
    like a well-tuned harp.

Julia Sovrin

MY MOTHER SPEAKING, IN HER AGE

I am old. I will die. I have the right,
in my own house, to pull up my dress,
and wade in the sunlight.
If I don't wind the clock,
it flowers back into the old days.
There is no harm, now.

You can't live alone anymore, said the doctor.
*Whom do you love? With whom
will you live? Where do you want to go?*

I love my brother, and Roland.
Where is your brother? asked the doctor.
Dead.
And who is Roland? I don't know.

But I remember
we came home from school, our way,
around the barn,
climbing the back yard windmill;
each day, the forbidden leap
from windmill to roof,
through Dad's bedroom
and down the back stairs.

And I remember
my tennis ball
smacked against the dark, truthful red
of the barn wall. The far reach,
like the leap from windmill to roof.

And I remember my collies,
running to me through a sea of light
that was the fruit orchard.
I remember their great fur ruffs
in my arms' embrace.

No. I will not live with indifference.

If I must stay with my daughters,
or women who are old, like me,
I will kill myself. Or else,
live among them, ironical to the bone,
never telling of me and my brother and Roland
climbing the windmill,
or the smack, smack, smack of my tennis ball
against the red barn,
or whistling my collies home.

Ann Goldsmith

SPRING ON THE FRONTIER

Last year's skirt will not close,
Neither will the barn door.
My children will kill themselves
Trying to ride the goats. My husband
Wants to get out of here.
Every April the same.
He heard the honkers yesterday
At milking time: so full of news
You would have thought
They'd bring out the leaves to listen.
We rot too long indoors,
Crouching like animals, dirty and chilled,
Hoarding light, hungry for space,
The barnyard filling with snow
Like a bucket with milk from the cow.
Such winters are not good for family life.
I could leave them all,
Not to go far, just through the woods
To the waterfall, to sit on a rock
And breathe in the sharp sweetness

Of earth and pines, and rest my back.
Those geese are barking like a pack of hounds.
No wonder my husband fingers his rifle.
No wonder the children jump in puddles.
They say they lost their balance, he says
He'll fix the barn door right away.
April makes liars of us all.
But what heaven to roll up my sleeves
And hang sheets in the sun!
They buck like colts and my heart
Leaps like a fish.
Nothing can hold it down today.

Juanita Tobin

LAST WORDS

Her children seed continents.
The last great grandchild
flew in on a pillow
to be blessed with an accent
that knocks out a green flag.
Under eyebrows like awnings,
a smile cracks her face
as the sun cracks a stone.
She rattles from house to garden
where the goat is tied,
gives everything away except
the grandfather clock,
handcarved oak with Edison's head
in gold on the pediment,
a gift from her husband
they bought at Tiffany
on their first anniversary.

He was the head of the house
but she was the neck

and could turn his head
anyway she liked.
Her children won't get the clock
until her time runs down.
If there's a hairpulling match,
they'll feel her toe
in her shoe from below.
What else was there to do
but wind the clock,
feed the goat,
have a cup of tea;
think about the bone factory?
Time didn't stop until
she fell asleep writing
   I'm as old as God.

Justine Buisson

BUTTONS

   The Daughter

When Mother died they went
to me. All kinds. I rinse
my fingers with them, dredge up
gold and silver, pearls.
Shirt buttons I can use.
One always turns up that matches,
or nearly.
My favorite is the ivory flower.
I put it on a chain. The enamelled one
would make perfect earrings if there were two.

   The Mother

She's kept almost all and added
a few: buttons I clipped

when her father's shirts gave out;
an enamelled one from the dress
I wore to the speakeasy when he was out of town.
"Do you love Daddy
as much as Uncle Jack?"
Her accusing eyes.

The Grandmother

Some of these were mine:
the ivory edelweiss is one of ten
that corseted my wrists
on Sundays. They used to break
my fingernails.
We were patient
in those days.

The Buttons

We outlast the hands
that fasten us, lose us,
pick us up. We don't change
much, keep quiet about our origins.
When this woman lets go
others will find us.
Pry us loose from sediment of sunken
rooms, hang us on a string,
sew us to cloth not yet
woven or colored or cut,
turn us around in the light.

Jeanne Elliott

BUY THE LARGE SIZE

Five pounds of honey for a single teaspoon
in afternoon tea for one,
a case of tomato sauce that must be unpacked,
bottom tins used before more pile up.
Take a dozen of the special,
the largest size of anything
that can be kept for half a year.
In a city apartment, two bedrooms, no garage,
a hundred yards from the nearest store,
groceries gather, lured by an inaudible piper.
The freezer cradles nut-meats, lemons, casseroles, cheese.
Jars of beans and macaroni line the counters;
tea and coffee cluster on the upper shelf.
On rainy nights they sing quietly to themselves,
and in my blood the chorus echoes:
It was a long winter long ago,
weeks and weeks of cabbage and cornbread.

Jean Hollander

END OF MEMORY

What can I bring you
after ten long years?
If you had lived
you would have been
too old for tears.
I pluck a sprig of purple flowering
that dried all winter and I set
it broken in the crust of snow
where deer have hoofed
embroidery of nightly visiting
around your stone.
From horror that remains
I raise you tall as I
your otherness, blue eyes, blond hair,
against my dark, having forgotten all
the details of your face except
your head against my neck
and that my last consoling was
to wash your things as though
you still could wear.

Leona Mahler-Sussman

BLESS THE PEBBLE ON THE ROAD

Given a plunging roadway
a skidmark forty feet long
a tree transformed
into machete;

given headlights
hallucinating
last night's horror movie
car roof corrugated
windshield spawning
more fragments of glass
than could have sprung
from one frame;

given the cast and props
music sounding the
song of bones
the night blacker
blooded over with warm
spillage;

given the knot of panic
growing bigger than body
"I'm okay"
is hymnal
a gorgeous incantation
that meets on consecrated ground
black nights
blooded over;

given a daughter
lit with beauty
walking whole
I embrace all gods
honor the broken tree
bless the pebble on the road.

Alice Wirth Gray

CHILD IN FLIGHT

The auguries are good:
there's a rainbow.
I can see where both ends
come to earth. (Don't you).
Whichever end counts,
I relinquish my pot of gold.
It's a sacrifice, paid fare,
to the great god Heavier-than-Air.
A ray of sun shines on your DC-10,
that thin shell surrounding
my golden girl as the gold yolk
of an egg. Don't break
over Earth's bowl.

I don't laugh for anything
while you fly. All my levity
is to bolster you up.
I don't think about the future
when you're up in the air.
I do exercises to rid myself
of hubris.

Sucked through the hatch door
when the cabin depressurized
and never found. Or small pieces
spread over an area three miles around
and fire too. This list goes on and on.
My heart swells like a balloon,
my dear, dear heart, until you land
mine won't burst. Truly, then I say,
See? I carried you there.

Charlotte Alexander

SOMEWHERE IN ERIE, PENNSYLVANIA

Somewhere in Erie, Pennsylvania
the baby lies,
hydrocephalic

swaddled
in intensive care
until it will die
("it is only a matter of time").

I saw you in May,
and you told me more than anyone ever had
with your fingers, with your voice,
about that mysterious shape,

that ever more ambiguous choice,
which I knew, still,
you would never unmake.

I lingered, childless yet sisterly,
in the shadow of your bigness,
always laboring
to know the unsentimental truth,

wishing to protect,
like some fierce Ruth,
yet wanting not to show
I was afraid.

Two springs we had already seen
with you nearing term;
lilacs and picnics
and all your neat pots and seeds
waiting:

two babies dead.

And now this third floats out there
detached and lonesome
from your safe accord,
unknowing
how we wait.

Where did this all begin?
How much more technology can we afford?

Oh, Christie, I would kill for you
if they'd but let me in!

Francine Ringold

MY MOTHER

My mother was a high woman.
She sat up tall in bed,
pillows piled behind her back.
Some days she'd fall
if the sheets weren't pulled tight,
and we didn't place her right
in the middle of the pillows so
the hollow would hold her bones.
But she was tall.
And she'd say:
Bring me old news
and spread it out;
bring me potatoes, the knife,
an onion—a few carrots.

And right there in her pillows
she'd carve up the stew
order it set on the stove
steaming.

Sometimes, at night, even now,
I feel something press
down the edge of my bed
next to my chest.
I say to myself:
hold still. Don't breathe.
I keep my eyes shut.
I feel the bed sink down.
I cross my arms over my chest.

That high woman holds me.

Janice Thaddeus

WEDDING FEAST IN THE FOREST OF COMPIÈGNE

While my husband and friends
pull wonders from the earth,
my citified eyes miss
the *Bûchons de Champagne,*
great blown mushrooms
fit for Führers or Queens,
and I can find only
the tiny améthystes,
scarily purple,
surely not edible,
yet bursting everywhere
in this thick low-growing
forest of Compiègne,
empty of men,
no crack of gun,
no train resting alone
with officials signing a score
of peace; no war—
only here and there
as our wedding friends
pluck the delicate food
I find a great round bowl,
fifty-year old
shell of a shell—
all that death
for the sake of death,
war for the sake of war—
and our gentle occupation,
food-gathering with friends,
enlarging our feast
with these wild gifts,
will leave no print,
no silent bowl
to commemorate hell.
Just so: love
is not history, and kisses
leave no marks.
Wild mushrooms eaten
join the unremembered acts
most unswervingly human.

Paula A. Roy

PASSAGE

I remember a Sunday
summer afternoon that wound
like ribbon
along a green canal
in Pennsylvania.
The narrow road slithered
so close to trees and shrubs
that twigs like green mice
scratched my forearm
where it lay sunburned and cool
along the car's door.
My left arm
sweated your shoulders;
your hair teased my wrist
like an itchy blanket.

I see my wrinkled lap
and feel the sweat sticky
where my thighs touch
and behind my knees.

When I look,
your profile blurs
against the slow canal, a mirror
full of fat leaves, paint smears
on a palette.
A shuttered house
on crayon stilts
leans in a kindergarten drawing
toward the lazy water;
now and then a quick breeze
snaps,
but mostly the day stands still.

The car glides faster than the water:
we roll like a dusty beetle
through the last green tunnel
into New Hope's yellow haze.

Helen Norris

WAKING

And while she slept from one to four
some holy word unspoke itself.
The noon world tilted on its axis
and its quaking, churning light
unwove her sleep and wove her waking,
breaking seal of eyelids shut
against the opened eye of day,
binding breath in drops that danced
upon the tightened drum of earth
and smelled of rust. Her bed was a shallow
boat marooned in sand. She heard
the beach sounds carried out to sea,
the blue sky drowning in the sea,
a nomad tern that skimmed its surface
sowing frenzied calls. She heard
the sun dissolving in the sand...
She grew afraid to look but then
she looked and saw her pale hand paler
on the sheet and saw the light
gone thin around her, saw him standing
by the door, his maleness more remote
and hostile to herself, his love
unraveled in the room, his joy
unraveled in the room... Her mouth
was salt. The past was a fleck of sea
foam she had tasted while asleep.
The years before them crâshed upon
her like a wave that crushed her breath.
You slept, he said. *I dreamt,* she said,
that things were different, and she turned
from him and wound the sea-changed years
around her like a shell
or like a shroud.

Harriet Susskind

IN A WHEAT FIELD MAPPED LIKE KANSAS

October. Coveys of leaves cross the road.
You run the first length hard and fast
until the edges of breath
catch like spiked teeth in the hedge row
snaring the tail of my jersey.
We climb over logs stacked in a pile
into the clearing in a wheat field
mapped like Kansas.
We've gone far past the three mile limit.
You take me slowly back to the road.
Truckers inside their silver cabs
yell something, a flack of syllables:
Atta girl honey, burn the bum up,
then spin off and down the gulley.
Their cries carry me beyond pain
and this necklace of sweat.
My limbs move in some familiar joy
as I cover the miles with you.
We've come back to our rectangular field.
Early spring trillia thrive, and in summer,
bells of sweetpeas climb. Spindles of wheat
shiver in the first catch of sun.
I want us to begin and end like this—
a field coming through the seasons
bearing urgency like flowers—
a harvest that gives everything
to winter in absolute light.

Mildred Cousens

THE EGRETS

Three white egrets stood in the morning marsh,
motionless as figures stenciled upon glass,
their stemlike legs deep in the chill black water,
beaks all pointing across the open landscape
beyond the murky water, the wild morass.

Three white egrets, scarcely believable,
pure as Platonic virtues though less rare,
still as if waiting for a sign or signal
till from the tall pine grove a fourth one flew,
wheeling and circling in the sunlit air

over the others till they came alive,
lifted their beaks, fan-spread their folded wings,
forsook at last the dark primeval water,
wheeled and circled, then following their leader,
soared and flew in ever lessening rings
toward an unknown, yet somehow known horizon—

I called him courage for a human reason.

Kaela Petrov-Levine

SHEVUOS ON CAMPUS

It is time for the flutes
to herald the bringing of first fruits
to the temple....

    Under the leaves
    that curve like shoulders
    the plaza is clear
    in the wake of the day.
    The performers,
    the true believers,
    the working survivors
    have gone.
    Corners and bites of litter
    scurry like crabs
    over old brick in the breeze.

    A young man sits
    on the eastern steps.
    Beneath his hat
    his nose is painted
    solemn black.
    The woman leaning on his thigh
    plucks her guitar,
    low, slow in the sun.
    A white dog lies
    impassive as Egyptian stone
    at the hem of her coat-of-Joseph gown.

    Against a tree
    a white-shirted boy
    draws from his recorder
    a sweetwood melody.

    Under a portico across the square
    three chanters draped in orange
    tap bare feet
    on the shadowed stone,
    ring and tap in the drowsy air sing

hare hare
bells and drum.

.... the time of the flutes
has come.

Natalie Nelson

FIRE KITES

Long ago, on nights like this,
when the lake was flat black solid,
invisible except where lights from the other shore
lay on the surface like fine spun fishing lines,
the children came begging paper, pins and matches,
our permission, to build and fly the flaming fire kites.

Fire kites were single sheets of newsprint,
corners pinned, enclosing air within a paper husk.
When lit correctly as they always were, they rose high
into the dark and humid night, lighting children's faces,
causing breath-held hush to fall on all of us.
When the pin burned free, the kite raised wings
and hovered, challenging the dark with soundless flame.

On nights like this,
when the lake is soft black velvet, nearly flat,
I take a paper, pins and matches to the sandy shore
to build and light one fragile fire kite.
There are no children left to fly the craft
and I have need to see the burning ash descend,
red lace carbon flakes of glowing wings
drifting over water, cooling, dim,
like tissue-thin black final birds
come to spend a final night by me.

Maud Marshall

ELEGY

for Marian Buehler

On this day of your death, the buds
of filigree fanning above the elms
harden in sleet and drop at my feet.
A blue grosbeak flutters at the feeder,
afraid to land.

I have cut my finger on an envelope
with your name. The pain will not cease.
A cricket sings under my wastebasket.
I carry him to the dried ferns by the oak.

On this day of no breath, I divide
my daffodils, hundreds of them,
tiny like onion sets. I fill
all of the beds, but my fingers
are too cold to make the holes deep.

The kitten comes from next door.
He skitters away when I try to touch him
and races across the street.
Brakes squeal and I cover my eyes.
When I open them, he is pruning his tail
beneath the weeping hemlock.

On this day the sun sets, the shades
of its fingers stretch back to the east
in all of the colors you wore. The star
I wished on glitters cold and bright.
A Canada goose glides low by itself,
calling.

I fix a pot of Earl Grey tea and pour it
in Aunt Mini's fragile cup. You said
the hospital made coffee by dangling a bean
over the pot and boiling hell out of the shadow.
I smile, but afterward my lips are stiff
and ashamed.

On this day I am left, I understand
when Schweitzer said influence of example
was not the most important thing—
it was the only thing.

Today the catheter cannot find my heart.
I could look into the sun without blinking.

Coco Gordon

AFTER 41 YEARS
I FIND A WINDOW IN MY TABLE:
IT GIVES ME COURAGE

You sit to eat. Trust the image,
what you see, I am in your table.
Say to me, No, there will be no more
babies for any man's thirst and say,
Yes alone you will give more life
than every bud on this privet thrown to you.
Eat through the path I make
which accents the emptiness of all the chairs.
I am the setting across from you.
Every day the flags in me blow,
sometimes east, sometimes they tangle
on Mr. Gay's pole, he never pulls them in
at night, they are in shreds and blossoms
are gone on the cherry. But why am I
telling you this, you just have to
sit here alone to see it.
Eating alone's not so terrible.
What is that triple beam balance
scale doing in my image, I barely see
frets of maple in its platform.
I understand you wanting to sink
into work when the table's not in use

for eating, but it, too, is using the table,
pushing my border of deliverance out,
taking over as it gets dark.
If you haven't heard me and you are still
sitting there, or have gotten up
and have come back the next day,
I will be here bright as day allows,
telling you life isn't so bad if you have a table
to look into, the omnipresent sound
of sill in it holding down a tree
grafted with limbs of air. Out is in
and with you, out as you can follow it,
much depends on the weather for that
and the fact that you choose to sit here at all.
Eating standing up is a sure deterioration
of image, well-being, digestion,
all sorts of things you shouldn't
let happen when you're alone, even if the food
tastes better cold and an extra slice of bread
more easily buttered. Why I've been here
every day shining like a revelation
but you haven't noticed me till today,
for the first time soothed by my calling you in
with high frequency assurances.
I can't take you by force, I am a *passive* image,
all I can do is be here talking to you repeatedly
with the branch of maple filling the pane
till it cuts off my breath with summer.

Geraldine C. Little

ILLUMINATIONS: FISH

They hang under ice
as if asleep, in dreams

hearing perhaps
the sink of limb shadows,

from a mirey womb, fantasies
of peeper eggs imagining what

they will become, fronds
moaning at moon-knock, a stone

shifting in something like wind
more like remembrance of wave.

Their heads may sing with sound
in that tingled globe.

It is always the way,
silence an illusion

like frost in the bone
already phrasing: *flowers*

Harriet Susskind

THE LESSON OF THE PHOENICIAN

I see you pace the worn Aubusson
then stretch your arms behind your back
in the beamed attic of your brownstone.
You look down from the fifth floor
towards turn of the century houses.
Their roofs zig and zag in the haze
of Manhattan. Coffee bubbles on an

ancient stove. Stacked on your scrivener's
desk, the new long poem, complete at last.
In my own quarters I pour hot water
over a tea bag, amazed at the tawny yield
and the scent that turns one form into another.
In this morning of ignorance and cold
something is coming of age.
I didn't know the art of the old masters,
the history of the Phoenicians—
close relatives to Moabites and Hebrews.
You, good scholar, spend hours in half
dark of the city libraries, mastering
the fine print. When you write
all the past opens its doors,
cold latch springs come to life.

Here, I try to move small pockets of facts.
I arrange uncertain years as if
there were a history in that.
Then I sit imagining you tall, a dandy
in an uncarpeted room, and barefoot.
I try to remember the well-trimmed beard.
I try to hear you call me back into that room
to see a wine glass balanced crazily
and your fingers making whale music
on its rim. Then I remember
your arms circled around me in sleep.

I see only how the new year begins
in new snow like a false heart.
In shops all over this town, paper
weights have gone on sale.
I can't resist flipping their silent contents.
I telephone you over a long, long distance.
Not once do I speak the words I've collected.
Should you press your ear to my silence
then the sounds will form themselves.
Imagine the warm air of January and new snow
running ahead of us. Follow it.

Anneliese Wagner

PAINTER

A Woman in the Sun,
painting by Hopper

What happens before

Up from the bed, she reddens lips
lights a cigarette,
stands well in the room
facing the window, heels apart,
thighs full for him.

If he's too much boy
he'll crawl right under.

Coming near, his long fingers
plunge through curtain,
pave a citron morning
for her bare feet, his hand
a dress poured on her skin.

Breasts high as wings
widen for his blond head,
then fold, shield him to her.

What happens during

Eyes closed she opens
the single eye of her knees.

His first entry into a woman ready
heat floods into heat
for however long. . .
she holds his white light.

When he slips off
her bamboo legs grow on floorplanks,
slide up the wall,
stripe a painting.

What happens after

Arms lifting she inhales
his salt coating her body,
smooths her yellow hair,
lights a cigarette.

A fallen shoe, a standing shoe
wait by the rumpled bed.

She does not turn to watch
through the east window
as he brush-kisses trees,
rushes across hills.

In the room her life
begins with paint, with yellow
years, years of skimming fat,
the reach toward white.

Carol R. Hackenbruch

WAR GAMES

I danced loud circles,
wanted red paint,
drums, scalps.

Father stopped my run,
corrected my dance.

See, small shuffles,
no full steps,
or knees flying.
Calm your voice.
Their dance was proper
just so, just so.
Their worship was song
to Sun, Water, Earth.

He muttered Sioux
and held up their sky.
He layered grass with buffalo,
talked yellow sand and red water,
marks on maps,
walkers of slow circles.

Jill Breckenridge Haldeman

TRANSMUTATIONS

Cancer is shrinking my tall father.
Our voices hush as he grows smaller,
I grow younger: a college girl
again, showing him my dorm—
the plaid curtains, the matching spread.

Running back home from grade school,
white dots bouncing on my navy dress,
I bring him straight A's.
In my playpen, I babble
Daddy's girl, while he leans
on his black cane in my huge baby hand,

the hand that cannot hold him
in his skin and bones. Dropping back
to embryo, I'll sail that glassy stream
toward the luminous union,

while my father, in a distant sky,
soars upward by the thousands.

Janice Thaddeus

THE VOYAGE OUT

Thirty years ago we chose to go along
when I was nine, and our farm
had just slipped under.
I remember how my father
stood that night among his cows in the barn.
It was Christmas, with
Venus so bright that it looked like the True Star,
and we stood in the straw,
my father and I,
listening,
the cat rumbling warm on our shins.
A man never got enough of a chance
to be alone with his cows,
he said, and held me against him
in the fertile barn smell.
There's no money, so we've got to be heroes,
to leave the cows and the night,
go where it's always day, and the earth's
just a blue smudge in a black sky.

That was the year they promised me a new world
for Christmas.

I was nine, and bolts of excitement
clanged in me louder than the thrust of lift-off
or the trip to this great station.
We are not alone. Five others gleam
around us. Down on earth, they say,
so many millions starve,
their thin images grimacing on the television,
that they're planning to shoot a few
beyond the moon.

We feed our garbage to rabbits,
lots of flesh and very little bone,
very eatable animals, rabbits:
everything here is purposeful, human,
bread grown from stalks in styrofoam.

We carol the myth of Christmas.
I try to describe the black night, stars, straw.
I was only nine.
My son pokes at the styrofoam,
praises my rabbit pie.
What bleak imaginings!

When my father died we divided his innards
relegating his guts, bone, brain
in the useful way we've invented here,
for posterity and progress.
Remember, Lena, he whispered at the last,
*The warm cows in the barn at night,
remember the grass.*

This is the voyage.

Remember the unplanned delicacy of spring,
a million toad-eggs, clamor of night song,
none of it for us,
tadpoles, all head, ringing the pond,
so much extra life and death,
all the wastage of surprise.

Here no thrush sings, no jays scatter
nuthatches or chickadees.
Sometimes I sit in the zoo and dream,
sit with my caged children.

Norma Westwood

THE FARM: BLUE MORNING LIGHT

Released from the timeless wrestling
of a dream, you wake to the slow
clothing of the mind: put on
the blue morning light,
the stiff epaulets of the hours.

Still fumbling for focus,
you know that you will never
catch up; step across
the grass past the well, whose image
fills the hollow behind

your eyes. Its stones, its water
pull you back; how
did the ancients feel, looking
down, seeing their faces
floating like ghosts from a lost

island? Only later
you might see,
with a disorientation like fear,
what your face in the water is:
a blind stare, from a wrinkle

of eyes, mouth, hair,
drowned in the pool of sky.
Looking up, you see
that time is a wide field
you will always gaze across,

the near grain too close
for clarity, the tiny figures
of a thin old man,
a running dog, barely
visible on the other side.

Patricia Hooper

DEER IN THE OPEN FIELD

1

They are there from the beginning.
Sometimes they move toward you,
shyly, until you notice.
Long ago, as a child, you saw them
and followed their tracks for hours
through deep grass. Finally
you knew you had lost them and stood
farther off than you intended,
grass stretching in every direction
and none of it bent or parted
to show where the deer had vanished.
It was late evening, and far
in the distance you saw your house
the size of a stone, and your brothers
enter and shut the door
on the field forever.

2

Many things choose you: grass
harnessed in sunlight, leaves
stammering, stones
hushed in a courtyard.

And always the wildflowers,
their bodies blowing like seas,
simple as water.

You know them.
But the others who come toward you
with their field-breath, their furred antlers,
you love more.

When they nuzzle your hand
they are saying *Name me,* their bodies
pleading, their eyes like your eyes,
lucid and vulnerable.

3

Their season. Again the crimson
maples, the hills ignited,
the seeds frantic.

And milkweed—
where shall it set down
its mild cargo?

As on a battlefield
a creature should give birth,

so the pods open
releasing
a weightlessness unasked for,
like the soul's,

till, in the mud,
the seeds, barely visible,
writhe from their tents of feathers.

And overhead
gunshot,
the startled animals,

a field of husks.

4

You wait for a long time
in your life, which you were given.
Finally a door opens:
you step forth from the house
and there is the sun, already
sweeping the field, and trees
whose names you had not forgotten,
fastened in frost like armour,
so dazzling, so inventive

you know you will walk toward them
in spite of the wildflowers
asleep in their glass prisms
and the sky, bone-white, unentreating.
You see them, not far off,
gathered, their antlers lifted
from the deep grasses, in welcome.
While back of you, as before,
the dust wakes on the doorsill
and light touches the wall
as it did so many times
when you were living.

Phyllis K. Collier

BOARD BY BOARD

It goes in a circle, this island.
The roads cross over
each other like loose ropes with no
ends. At the ferry two sisters
bring two-by-fours. Later they will pound
their nails into the firm flesh of the wood,
keeping time. The bubble in their level
will oil its way to dead center.

It is warm enough now for the fawns
to trip down out of the bracken,
for the iris to unfold. The two women
sling boards, their soft arms flashing
white as gulls. Their bodies blur
with their rhythms. At evening the one sister
starts the potatoes. The print of their scarves
comes into focus as they pause to look out
over the trillion waves.

NOTES

Editors

RACHEL HADAS is a poet and critic whose work has appeared in many periodicals including *Parnassus, Yale Review, The New Republic, The New Yorker* and *Virginia Quarterly Review.* She teaches English at the Newark campus, Rutgers University.

CHARLOTTE MANDEL has published poetry, short fiction, and critical essays in such journals as *Iowa Review, Greenfield Review, West Branch,* and *Women's Studies.* Her first collection of poems, *A Disc of Clear Water,* was published 1981 by Saturday Press.

MAXINE SILVERMAN's poetry has appeared as a chapbook, *Survival Song* (Sunbury Press, 1976) and in the anthologies *Pushcart III: Best of the Small Presses* and *Voices Within the Ark: Modern Jewish Poets.* She is poetry editor of *Response: A Contemporary Jewish Review.*

Contributors

CHARLOTTE ALEXANDER's poems appear in *Prairie Schooner, Carleton Miscellany, Niagara Magazine.* She is editor of *Outerbridge,* and teaches at College of Staten Island (CUNY).

JUNE RACHUY BRINDEL has published fiction and poetry in *MSS, Iowa Review, Story Quarterly,* as well as a children's book, and a first novel, *Ariadne: A Novel of Ancient Crete.*

LOVERNE BROWN is a former Alaskan, now living in California, who writes engineering and educational manuals for a living.

JUSTINE BUISSON has published poetry in *Kansas Quarterly, Cimarron Review, Nimrod.* She also writes fiction and teaches creative writing in Miami Adult Education Program.

ELLIN CARTER coordinates a women's poetry workshop, teaches science fiction, and edits a weekly poetry column in Columbus, Ohio.

ROBERTA CHESTER has published poems in *Penumbra* and *Visions.* She teaches writing at College of the Atlantic, Bar Harbor, Maine.

PHYLLIS K. COLLIER works for Boeing Aerospace where she writes, mostly about airplanes.

MILDREN COUSENS has had poems published in such magazines as *The American Scholar, Saturday Review, Hudson Review.*

SHEILA COWING is author of an award-winning children's book about wetlands ecology. Her poems appear in *Tendril, Tar River Poetry, Georgia Review.*

ELAINE DALLMAN's poems appear in *Epoch, The Chowder Review,* and many anthologies. She is chief editor for *Woman Poet* regional anthology series.

NANCY DAVIES is on the Literature faculty of Maharishi International University in Fairfield, Iowa.

SANDRA DEMAREST is enrolled in the MFA program at University of

Arizona; she writes both poetry and short fiction.

PATRICIA DOBLER's book of poems, *Forget Your Life,* will be published as a winner of *Annex 21:* American Poetry Series Contest (University of Nebraska).

SUSAN DONNELLY was feature poet in the Spring/Summer 1982 issue of *Soundings East,* and poetry editor of the Summer 1981 issue of *Dark Horse.*

SHELLEY EHRLICH's chapbook of poems, *How the Rooted Travel,* is forthcoming from Juniper Press. She does psychiatric social work, teaches, and edits.

RUTH F. EISENBERG's poems appear in *Connecticut River Review, Voices International, Laurel Review.* She teaches at Pace University, Pleasantville, N.Y.

JEANNE ELLIOTT teaches English in San Jose, California. She is influenced by her Nebraska childhood, the Victorian period, and feminist literature.

BARBARA EWELL grew up in northwest Tennessee. She teaches English at Radford University, in Radford, Virginia.

ANN GOLDSMITH teaches poetry writing workshops in Erie and Niagara County schools under auspices of ALPS (Alternative Literary Programs in the Schools).

COCO GORDON is a poet/papermaker/visual performance artist/founder of Water Mark Papermill and Press. She makes environments/installations in which she performs her poetry, notably "Piano-Trap with Suite of Poems for John Cage." This performance was part of a major solo at Central Hall Artists in New York City.

ALICE WIRTH GRAY lives in Berkeley, California. She has published poetry and short stories, and has written a novel.

CAROL R. HACKENBRUCH's poems appear in *Cedar Rock, Great Lakes Review, Green River Review.* She is associate editor of *Passages North.*

JILL BRECKENRIDGE HALDEMAN's poetry appears in *Noeva: Three Women Poets* and elsewhere. She won a 1977 Minnesota State Arts Board Grant, and a 1980 Bush Foundation Fellowship.

PHEBE HANSON has toured with Minnesota Poetry Outloud. She teaches at Minneapolis College of Arts and Design.

ANNE HARTER-JONES has a degree in music, plays cello, viola da gamba, and lute. She works part-time as a freelance journalist.

JEAN HOLLANDER's poems appear in *Sewanee Review, Quarterly Review of Literature, New England Review.* She is Poetry Editor of *The Princeton Spectrum.*

PATRICIA HOOPER's poems appear in *Ohio Review, Poetry, Chicago*

Review, Michigan Quarterly Review. She has taught at Wayne State University.

CAROLINE KNOX has published poems in *Poetry, American Scholar, Minnesota Review.* She is a college English teacher in Connecticut.

BARBARA LANGHAM's poetry, fiction and essays appear in *North American Review, Fiction Texas, Sing Heavenly Muse, Poetry Now.*

ANN Z. LEVENTHAL's poems, short fiction and essays appear in *Crow Call, The Vanderbilt Review.* A play was produced by the West End Arts Council in Hartford, Conn.

GERALDINE C. LITTLE has won four major awards from The Poetry Society of America, and is widely published. She is President of Haiku Society of America.

LEONA MAHLER-SUSSMAN is a freelance writer/artist. She has lectured and given demonstrations throughout the states.

MAUD MARSHALL writes short stories in addition to poetry. She has written a thesis, "Art and War in Protest Poetry."

NATALIE NELSON lives in Minnesota where she has been writing poetry seriously since 1971.

HELEN NORRIS has published two novels. She has spent almost all of her life in Alabama; has taught English in college.

GHITA ORTH is the winner of the Eileen W. Barnes Award for her collection, *The Music of What Happens,* published 1982 by Saturday Press. She teaches at University of Vermont, Burlington.

KAELA PETROV-LEVINE's poems appear in *Berkeley Monthly, Leanfrog, View from the Top of the Mountain, A Bell Curve of Reason.*

LISA RESS has published poems in *Kalliope* and *Columbia.* She is working on her MFA in Creative Writing at Cornell where she is a teaching assistant.

FRANCINE RINGOLD is editor of *Nimrod,* has taught at University of Tulsa, currently produces radio programs in the humanities. Her poetry and fiction appear in *Texas Quarterly, Southwest Review.*

PAULA A. ROY chairs the English Department at Westfield Senior High School. Her work appears in *Middle Jersey Writers Anthology* and professional journals.

MARY KAY RUMMEL has published poems in many Midwest journals. She teaches at University of Minnesota, and spends much time in the North Country.

ELIZABETH ANNE SOCOLOW lives in Princeton, N.J. and teaches writing in schools, workshops, private homes, corporations, universities.

JULIA SOVRIN has published poetry in *Chelsea, New York Quarterly.* She has worked as a journalist and editor, and is writing a novel.

HARRIET SUSSKIND has published poems in *Mid-American Review,*

Connecticut Quarterly, Georgia Review. She teaches English at Monroe Community College, Rochester, N.Y.

JANICE THADDEUS has published in *Atlantic, Shenandoah, Michigan Quarterly Review.* She teaches poetry writing at Barnard College.

JUANITA TOBIN is a retired psychiatric nurse. She was awarded a 1981 grant from New Jersey State Council on the Arts.

ANNELIESE WAGNER has published poems in *Ploughshares, Poetry Now, Greenfield Review, West Branch.* She has been awarded several fellowships at Yaddo and The MacDowell Colony.

LOIS V. WALKER has published poems in *College English, Xanadu, Phoebe.* She is chairperson of Long Island Poetry Collective, and is a visual artist.

KATHERINE WELLS has published work in *Kayak, Colorado-North Review, California State Poetry Quarterly.* She is a graphics artist.

NORMA WESTWOOD is a former social worker. Her poems are published in a variety of little magazines.

ELIZABETH WILLIAMS teaches creative writing at University of Wisconsin—Milwaukee. She is published in *The Anglican Theological Review, Cream City Review, Wisconsin Poets' Calendar.*

BARBARA WINDER teaches at Western Connecticut State College. Her poems appear in *Kansas Quarterly, College English,* and she has won the Wilory Farm Poetry Prize.

ANN WOOLFOLK's poems appear in *Berkeley Poets Cooperative Anthology* and *U.S. #1 Poets.* She was awarded a grant from New Jersey State Council on the Arts for poetry and graphics.